The Joy of Writing

An Exploration of the Art of Writing in Prose

Ralph Hipps

Table of Contents

Introduction

Do you remember that scene in *Finding Nemo*? The one where Dory tells her friend, the dejected Marlin, to 'just keep swimming?' Well, this is what I say to you: if your mind feels like porridge; if the *mot juste* seems as elusive as a dream; if you feel about as creative as a vacuum; well, just keep writing. Write through the inelegance! Write through the clunkiness! For there is light, my friend, at the end of the tunnel. And there is joy to be had in verbal creation. There is nothing better -- to my mind -- than the joy of writing. This is my paean to writing.

Why, you might ask, is writing such a felicity? The answer is not so simple. One might say, 'There is joy in a well-turned phrase, or a clever *bon mot*; there is joy in the dissection and articulation of a feeling.' For me, however, there are deeper joys to be had; such joys have more to do with spiritualism, with connection to a kind of collective unconscious; which exists in us all. Through writing we fall into a dream. Sometimes, upon rereading a page of my prose, I am struck by a sense of wonder: I wonder where the words even came from: it is as if I were actuated, temporarily, by an alien energy. When you enter this space, when you feel as though --

4

no longer bound by the parameters of ego, transcendent of the self -- anything is possible, you realise that writing is, at best, a spiritual activity. When you enter this space, you begin to comprehend creation. That is, you begin to comprehend how the human being, though once foraging in forests, developed agriculture; built houses; flew to the moon. You begin to comprehend the process of generation. You enter this space very seldom; but there is nothing quite like it.

So, if you wish to access, for a moment, a cosmic consciousness; if you wish to draw from the well of life: well, just keep writing. Do not give free rein to self-loathing! We are prone to this. We derogate ourselves for the slightest errors. A little bit of self-loathing, unfortunately, is necessary; a little bit of anxiety is energising; but not too much: make sure to rein it in. Do not allow it to retard your progress: just keep writing. Do not throw yourself onto the bed muttering, 'I'm an idiot! I'm an idiot! I'm an idiot!' You are not an idiot. You do not fall within the zero to twenty IQ bracket. You are simply imperfect. If you want to reach perfection: return to your writing! Amelioration occurs through repetition. Amelioration -- of both the style and substance of one's prose -- occurs through repetition.

There are those who privilege style; and there are those who privilege substance. But the good prosaist must straddle the line between the two: the good prosaist must self-question; must learn to marshal arguments, lest the prose should turn out shallow and incondite; and the good prosaist must, at the same time, attend to style; must ensure that the prose has rhythm; that sentences vary in length; that they persist to please the ear and please the eye. George Orwell advocates clarity; Walter Pater musicality. So: on the one side, you have George Orwell, to whom obfuscation is anathema, for whom language is, strictly speaking, a means to an end; and on the other side, you have Walter Pater, for whom prose need not be prosaic; might even be poetical; whose own sentences -- stuffed with parentheses and subordinate clauses -- are testament to his pursuit of verbal beauty. Orwell is to Pater what water is to whisky: for the former, prose serves simply to quench thirst; for the latter, however, prose serves to intoxicate. Orwell's "instrumental" attitude toward prose, his conception of prose as an expedient to signification, is at variance with Pater's "expressive" attitude. Prose, claims Pater, is an underrated medium. It can do much more than transfer a thought from mind to mind: it can give delight. It can infuse the reader with a certain *joie de vivre*. It can be flavourful, and jingling, and dynamic; it need not be flavourless, and toneless, and inert. Prose, claims Pater, is a mode of self-expression.

The truth is, though, that prose requires resistance: pressure forms diamonds; necessity mothers invention. That is to say, it is only when confronted with a challenge, when working within a framework, that the inventive faculty activates; and, just as the car needs a chassis, the piece of prose needs a structure. So, bearing this in mind, this is the structure of my humble little ebook: it comprises five parts -- part one deals with the joy of writing; part two with style and aesthetics; part three with substance and structure; part four with success and failure; and part five consists of the ten commandments of writing. The aim is creative pleasure; the question: 'How might I enter the space where anything seems possible?' The answer (in my humble opinion): 'One must develop, and hone, a style of one's own; one might find the right tone; one must give oneself a direction; and, last but by no means least, one must just keep writing.'

Chapter 1- The Joy of Writing

Why do we write? Renown? Do we write for renown? The renowned *homme de lettres* receives hundreds of letters a week; and it is their moral duty to reply to as many as possible. Fame is a double-edged sword. How about moolah? Perhaps we write for moolah? Dr Johnson certainly thinks so: 'No man but a blockhead,' he claims, 'ever wrote except for money.' But surely there are better ways of making moolah; surely there are easier ways, at least. Few and far between are those who support themselves solely by writing. So why write, then, if writing pays so badly?

Writing sometimes hurts you. It seems to expose your idiocy. You know nothing, apparently. You have forgotten everything you once knew. It is like getting blood out of a stone. Sentences come out in fits and starts. You know neither what you want to say nor how to say it. The journey from subject to predicate, from capital letter to full stop, is gruelling and joyless; it seems almost interminable; and you must expend all your energy, every last drop, in order to complete it. The sentence lies there unfinished, checking its watch, waiting impatiently for you to bring it home. But you cannot.

Eventually you complete it; then you reread it; then you repine. The end result, you think, is incommensurate with the time spent. You curse your maker: 'A pox on you,' you say, 'for creating out of muck such a schmuck as me.' You are in need of consolation. 'Life is inexplicable,' you tell yourself. 'Nothing matters. Everyone will die, and there is nothing we can do: according to Lord Calvin's second law of thermodynamics, the sun will burn out, and everything will turn to cinder. Nothing will survive. Our species, unless we have populated new galaxies by then, will die out; and the masterworks of our greatest artists - - the paintings of Picasso; the plays of Shakespeare; the novels of Joyce -- will turn to cinder. Nothing will survive. By now you have sunk into despondency. But you keep on writing -- whatever comes into your head -- and eventually, inexplicably, you rattle off a beautiful sentence. And you keep on writing. You practically let the words write themselves. You keep your fingers moving. And you enter the space of nullibiety. You don't look back. You stop rereading. You only look ahead -- into the mist.

You don't know where you are exactly. You're in the space between part and whole. You're kissing the cosmos.

Then you think: 'That is enough for now.' You reread it. You wonder where it came from. You are deeply satisfied. You reread it again. You like it less. You reread it once more, saying, 'Just let me take a run-up.' You get to where you stopped; you try to write; but nothing comes. You have lost the momentum. You must wrench fluency out of the fitfulness all over again. You just keep writing. The time spent between full stops contracts. You are advancing with decreasing effort. You can feel the wind on your cheeks. You are really moving. Life is wonderful. Here you are: an intelligent biped with opposable thumbs, sitting on a chair, looking at a screen, as the words of your mind find external form; in a house; in a town; in a country; on a planet -- of which a moon is in orbit -- in orbit of a star. Giant marbles, in outer space, are circling each other. Just because it happens to work like that.Just because it happens to work like that. The universe is weird and arbitrary. You are alive. You are aware of your own limitations. Unlike the animals (sunk in materiality), you (a body-spirit hybrid) find it all strange. Life is wonderful. You stop writing, You pick your nose. You wiggle your toes. You listen to your mother on the telephone; to her reassuring, deeply familiar voice -- the first voice you ever heard. You close your eyes; it is as if you never left the womb. You burp with your mouth closed. You open your eyes. You stare at the screen. You resume writing.

So: writing goes a little bit like this. It is a labour -- there is no doubt about that -- and sometimes it can seem Sisyphean; but it can be exalt you. And, beyond the superficial joys -- of having written something impressive, for example, something of which another writer would be jealous -- there is a joy in simply being; in being a part of something larger; which, for fleeting moments, writing has induced. There are moments when everything comes together, the universe around you seems to fall silent, and, adherent to the moment, you enter what I am calling the space of nullibiety. Life is long, and mostly bad, but such moments as these are redemptive.

Let me tell you what I did this morning: I woke up. I looked in the mirror. I thought, 'That is a bad face.' I opened up my laptop. I loaded up

Microsoft Word. I started writing. The writing went badly. 'This is joyless,' I thought, 'and I am an idiot. A member of the bad brigade, is what I am.' Then I took it out on the cursor: 'Look at this stupid cursor,' I thought, 'this winking vertical line. Stop winking at me, stupid vertical line.' The prosaist must be more than a prosaist: the prosaist must read extensively; must amass experiences; must assimilate discourse; must immerse himself in language; must keep a notebook in which to record details; must manage his personality; must like himself. The prosaist must be more than a good stylist, and a good grammarian: the prosaist must, primarily, be a good human being. Writing is a measure of personality; and unless you write out of a degree of self-love, you are unlikely to derive pleasure from the activity. You must readjust your self-conception. You must not look at yourself in the mirror and think, 'That is a bad face!' You must not read something by a contemporary and think, 'I wish I could write with such poise.' You must go and have a nap; or take a walk. You must go and spend some time in sylvan fields, amidst songful birds and burbling brooks. You must do a good deed. You must talk to your friend and make them laugh. You must see yourself through the eyes of one who likes you.

Then, and only then, may you return to your writing. Though some claim writing is a way of letting off steam, I have always regarded it as a kind of echo chamber: if I write out of anger, the anger seems only to exacerbate. Thus, writing works best -- that is, gives most joy -- when one's heart already contains some positive energy. Writing multiplies self-love.

Am I talking nonsense? I fear that I am. At least I am honest enough to say so. What it all comes down to, then, is this: there are such things as letters; letters combine to form words; words combine to form sentences; and so on and so forth. It all starts with the letter, then, the glyph. There are twenty-six of these in the Roman alphabet. They combine to form words. There are approximately one million of these in the English language. There are such words as -- let me just open my dictionary; bear with me a second -- so there are such words as "shindy" and "shebeen" and "shemozzle". "Shemozzle"? What a word! What a delightful little word! I am delighted. Yes, this is what delights me: the discovery and recalling -- especially the recalling -- of a beautiful word. I am a self-avowed logophile. Sometimes I remember nice big juicy ones. I fish for them in the waters of my mind. I can feel them take the bait. I bring them in. Sometimes -- alas! -- they get away from me. But sometimes I get a hold of them, and it is deeply satisfying. Let me try and remember a nice big juicy one; one that I have not used for a long time: how about "antediluvian"? Yes, that is a good one. You can try too! Try and catch a whopper! A polysyllabic monster! This is a hoot. Okay, perhaps I am overstating the amusement derivable from the activity. There is only so much fun to be had in remembering words in isolation. That is to say, the real pleasure comes from finding the right word at the right time; what Gustave Flaubert termed the *mot juste*.

It took Flaubert around five years to write *Madame Bovary*. According to his biographers, he would spend whole days shaping single paragraphs. Such writers as James Joyce, for whom not only the right words, but also the order of these words, was of signal importance, and William Butler Yeats, for whom a line would take 'hours maybe' to finish, are also remembered for the laboriousness of their writing processes. Such writers as these demanded a lot from their words: the word had to be both precise and euphonious; had to be both sonically and semantically suitable; had to have both style and substance to make the final draft.

We derive pleasure from euphony; and a fine piece of prose -- purified of aural irritants, organised with care -- is honey to the ears. The ear craves harmony; and rhyme; and tonal variety; without which it will tire, and cease to listen. The ear requires irregularity every so often as well: the best poets resort sometimes to the hypermetric line; and the prosaist, as well as the poet, must attend to sound; must train the ear; must let it lead the way. The vocable that fits the sonic pattern is preferable to that which does not. This might mean that the abstruse word is chosen over the simple one. Many writers -- acolytes of Orwell, for example -- will tell you to keep it simple at all costs; but if the sentence needs a certain number of syllables, and the simple word simply does not cut the mustard, then the writer will be well advised to close his eyes and think of synonyms; or if that does not work, to look in the thesaurus. It is sound, claims Robert Frost, that 'makes it fun to write and read'. If a man put a gun to my head and said, 'Which matters more: sound or sense?' I would have to chose the former.

I have no need for lollipops and spinning tops: I get my kicks from writing. Why do I write? For the same reason that I live: because it sometimes gives me pleasure. It depends on the time; on the place; on the quality of my face; but when the conditions are, as Goldilocks puts it, 'just right', I write with ease and transcend myself.

Chapter 2- Style and Aesthetics

What is style? Style is an expression of personality. Style is the stamp of self on structure. Style is neatness. Or the ability to make messiness seem neat. Style is self-confidence. Style is what makes reading pleasurable. Style is polish. Style is the difference between Honoré de Balzac and Gustave Flaubert. Style is the difference between Miguel Cervantes and Marcel Proust. Style is the difference between H. G. Wells and John Ruskin.

Let us consider a paragraph of John Ruskin's, a writer commonly praised for his good style, and determine what exactly makes it stylish. Here is one from *Modern Painters*:

As the strength of men to Giorgone, to Turner their weakness and vileness, were alone visible. They themselves, unworthy or ephemeral; their work, despicable, or decayed. In the Venetian's eyes, all beauty depended on man's presence and pride; in Turner's, on the solitude he had left, and the humiliation he had suffered.

The first sentence is economical: a less stylish writer might have said something like "Only the strength of men was visible to Giorgone; conversely, only their weakness and vileness were visible to Turner." Ruskin puts it more elegantly. Ruskin manages to say in (let me count) sixteen words what it would have taken (let me count) nineteen words for a less stylish writer. He omits the word "were" in the second sentence: he omits wherever he can; and he is sparing in his use of conjunctions. Like most good writers, he makes his words work overtime: in the first sentence, for example, the word "were" is working for two clauses. Thus, economy of expression is a mark of good style.

What else? How about the arrangement? Ruskin's prose certainly necessitates syntactic unravelling. He chops up, rearranges his sentences to form interesting patterns. Anticipatory of the likes of Henry Green, who, in the words of Graham Greene, jostles the structure of his sentences 'like the scraps of paper in a kaleidoscope', Ruskin's sentences rarely advance in straight lines. Ruskin regarded prose as "word-painting", and the movement of his sentences, their to-and-fro tortuosity, evokes the movement of the paint brush on the canvas.

Kind of. Thus, intricate syntax is a mark of good style.

What else? How about rhetorical devices? Ruskin alliterates often (e.g., "despicable" and "decayed"); he also uses assonance (e.g., "eyes" and "pride"). His style is often regarded as biblical, moreover, for his use of parallelism (parallelism being the repetition of syntactical constructions for the sake of rhetorical effect). More specifically, he has a propensity to use anaphora and epistrophe (repetition at the front and back of sentences). Thus, the use of rhetorical devices conduces to stylishness.

How about flair? Flair connotes intuition; and zing; and spontaneity. Style is spontaneous; or, rather, has the semblance of spontaneity. Style is effortless; or, rather, has the semblance of effortlessness; necessitates, in fact, a lot of labour. But is this really the case? Perhaps we should look at it differently. Perhaps we should regard stylization not as labour, as do certain querulous contemporary writers, but as a form of play. The object of style is fun, not emphasis of meaning. Form *can* enact meaning (for example, one might employ an imbalanced sentence, one which falls with a bump, to emphasise a character's mental imbalance; or one might employ a pacy, pummelling sentence when discussing the effects of caffeine on a person), but meaning need not always dictate form. Style is, first and foremost, formal play; and the object of play is, first and foremost, fun. Children play with blocks; kittens with balls; chimpanzees with faeces; and writers with words.

So what is style, then? What have we learnt so far? Ruskin's prose is stylish, then, it seems. But need one write like Ruskin to be stylish? Not necessarily. Style exists in extremes. A simple well-made chair, displayed in the right light, might seem just as first-rate as a fancy throne. That is to say, a sentence need not be ornate, stuffed with decorative adjectives, syntactically tortuous, for it to be regarded as stylish. Thus, the prose of Hemingway is just as stylised as the prose of Updike. Though these writers are largely antithetical -- you would never catch Hemingway describing a socket, like Updike, as 'frowning' -- they are united by a conscious concern with shape. Roughly speaking: the more work one puts into one's prose, the more stylish it will be; and though Hemingway worked to pare down, not to elaborate, he is no less stylish a writer than the richly descriptive, mystifying Updike. Thus, style is both neatness and the ability to make messiness seem neat. Style is not simply floridity.

Style is not simply grammatical correctness, either. The stylish writer might even take certain liberties: might even get away with comma splicing (that is, joining two independent clauses with a comma). But I must add this caveat: only those writers in whom we trust, who can convince us that they are consciously flouting the rules, might get away with grammatical transgressions. Thus, style is self-confidence. Few can transgress with impunity. Most of us must abide by the rules of grammar, and must avoid the common traps, if we are to get published. Even the greatest of writers have been rejected because of grammatical incorrectness. Most famously, AndréGide rejected *Swann's Way,* the first volume of Proust's *In Search of Lost Time*, on account of finding a few grammatical errors. He came to regret his decision. But be warned: the editor may base their appraisal disproportionately on your grammar. Certain transgressions are permissible in the twenty-first century. For example: one might now begin a sentence with a conjunction. If one is writing a novel, moreover, one need not wrap one's dialogue in speech marks. But certain transgressions remain inexcusable. For example: the dangling participle is permitted under no circumstances. The participial clause must always refer to the subject. The linguist will tell you that language is an evolving organism, and that prescriptive grammar, in its attempt to fix, is fighting a losing battle. However, the editor is likely to have no time for the defence: "I was just advancing the English language." Do what the handbooks tell you! Get your prepositions right: it is "averse to"and not "averse *from*"; it is "different *from*" and not "different *than*".

Proust: 'Le style est tellement la marque de la transformation que la pensée de l'écrivain fait subir à la réalité.' This translates roughly as ("roughly" being the operative word): 'Style is really the mark of the transformation that the thought of the writer has made reality submit to.' What does this mean exactly? Style is perspective? Style is the personal language? Style is the way one makes a discipline one's own? If style is, as Proust implies, an imposition on reality, the suggestion is that reality does not want it. Its tendency is toward settlement. It does not want to change. Thus, a new style might first upset conservative readers; because it jars with their perspectives; because it is not what they are used to. (While I am writing this, this is what I am thinking: Where am I going here? What am I talking about? Who knows? Just keep writing.) So style is a new way of looking at reality. So reality is prey to construal. The individual, in the act of perceiving it, interprets it; and, in the act of interpreting it, transforms it; brings something fresh to it. (While I am writing this, this is what I am thinking: I am talking nonsense here. I am really talking nonsense.) So Proust is saying that style is a medium between the thought of the writer, the mind of the writer, and reality: that is, style is the lens -- or filter -- through which one sees the world. We might not realise that it is there; we might reread our prose and regard it as impersonal; but one's style is ineffaceable; and, though we are prone to forget it, we are looking at our lenses all the time.

Let us get to the essence of style: style is ... No, I've got no idea what Proust is talking about. I've got no idea what this sentence means. All I know is that it's pretty stylish. And this is an aspect of style: this almost-sense suggestive of profundity, provocative of thought. The good prosasist will resort to this every so often; will write such a sentence which, slightly raw, only three quarters of the way towards meaning, contrasts nicely with concreteness. From a textural standpoint, the prose may need an element of the wishy-washy. So long as it is contrasted with concreteness. But no. Surely it means something. Proust isn't really one to equivocate. Perhaps it will help to look at the quotation in context: it is from a paragraph denigrating Balzac, whom Proust compares unfavourably with Flaubert. According to Proust, the latter has an homogenous style. That is, his style acts as a kind of filter, purifying his vision of anything ugly; but Balzac, for Proust, is accepting of heterogeneity (it is for this reason that Mikhail Bakhtinfavours him). So Flaubert polishes, Balzac reflects, rusty reality. Style, therefore, is an idealisation of reality. Style is polish; style, in the case of Joesph Conrad, is Polish. Let us now discuss Joseph Conrad for a moment. I remember a scholar once saying something like, 'For a long period, following his retirement from the merchant navy, Conrad was without a profession; unless you count being Polish a profession.' This made me laugh out loud.

This brings me nicely to my next topic: the value of humour in prose writing. How was that for a segue! I segued via the Polishness of Conrad. That bears repeating: I segued via the Polishness of Conrad. Talk about tenuity! Okay then: I will discuss humour briefly before moving on to the topic of "aestheticism". So humour. We can think about it in terms of chiaroscuro: one needs the dark, but one also needs the light; one needs solemnity, but one needs some levity. One must vary things as much as possible; or at least have the taste to appreciate how much is too much. If you feel as though you are losing the reader's attention, you'd be well advised to resort to a joke or two. The sillier the better. If you are delivering a lecture, you should make the most of the visual element: wave your hands about or pull a face or something. Humour is just another flavour. And the perfect piece of writing is a melange of flavours, unified by style. Style is the grouping agent. Okay, that will do for today. I'm going to bed.

It is morning now. I slept well enough. I dreamt about an old schoolmate of mine, a small Jewish boy, who ended up being mauled to death by a dog in a supermarket. Anyway, it is time to discuss aestheticism in literature: this was a movement inaugurated by Walter Pater, to whom I have already referred in the introduction, whose aim was the evocation of pleasurable sensation. No longer was the aim simply the reflection of reality: the aim was now the idealisation of reality. The word "aesthete" comes from the Greek *aisthetes* ('one who perceives'). Thus, it has much to do with vision, and the ability to realise one's idealistic vision. Proust's description of Flaubert is the description of an aesthete.

For many, though, the aesthetic approach is reflective of a decadent society. When language serves no longer simply to express reality; when signifier comes unstuck from signified; then, according to GyörgyLukács, society is in a bad way. The writer has a deontic duty, claims Lukács; must raise a mirror to society, in order that the lower classes might see it for what it is and feel aggrieved about it; for Pater, however, the writer must simply give delight; must evoke 'as many pulsations as possible'. Life is brief and inexplicable, according to Pater; and so he advocates the pursuit of pleasing sensations. Given the elusiveness of actuality, and the brevity of one's interval, one must simply do what one enjoys. No one has a mission; no one has a duty. Life is not designed to hold together. So why waste one's time delaying its inevitable disaggregation? Such was the thinking process behind the aesthetic movement, whose rallying cry was 'l'art pour l'art'. (To throw a spanner in the works: Martin Amis claims that 'style *is* morality.' An unseemly sentence, he claims, is an affront to its reader. We shall look no further into Amis' somewhat sophistical statement. We shall move on.)

Chapter 3- Substance and Structure

If style is *how,* then substance is *what* one writes? So what should one write? That is the question. This is what Flaubert has to say on the matter: 'What I would like to create is a book about nothing, a book without external attachments held aloft by the internal force of its style.' According to the "spec screenwriter" Blake Snyder, however, 'a good movie has to be about something ... If you don't have a movie that's about something, you're in trouble.' Flaubert wished to write gorgeous nonsense, independent of the world from which it sprung, presided over by he its God-like author. Snyder says, 'Sounds like a big yawn.' Let's say we're writing a narrative. Does the narrative have to go somewhere? Must the character develop (fall from grace, for example, and change for the better)? Must there be some kind of hubristic decline? Perhaps one's point, though, is that the bad don't get their comeuppance; that the wicked avail themselves of wickedness. Must the story have a point; must one take a side; must one have a thesis in the first place? Of course, the what depends on the why: what we write depends on why we write. If we write for the sake of pleasing ourselves, then we need only appeal to our own sensibility. If we write for the sake of pleasing others, however, and thus pleasing ourselves by pleasing others, then we must appeal to the sensibilities of others.

What do they want? What do the people want? If they are anything like the Spice Girls, they may really reallyreally want to zig-a-zig-ahh! But anyway: they -- the brainless unknown -- want forwards movement. They don't want to stay in the same place for a hundred pages. But they don't want to move too precipitately either. They want to linger a little from time to time. They want to advance chronologically. They want to be able to follow what's going on. They don't want to jump back and forth. They are reading for plot. They are not students of literature. They want a point. They want there to be something at stake. They want to feel like they are investing their time in something worthwhile. They want a likable protagonist. They don't want to spend their time in the company of a blackguard, a sinner without redeeming characteristics. They want to go, 'That's so true.' They want to go, 'That's pretty clever.' They want to go, 'That's hilarious.' They don't want to go, 'That's different.' So, in order to please these people: follow the following rules!

The narrative consists of set-up, conflict, and resolution. One needs an antagonist; one needs a hero; and one needs a victor. The same holds true for an essay: one needs an argument; one needs a counter-argument; and one needs a resolution. In this sense, incidentally, a plot is similar to a game: a football match, for example, might be understood as a kind of plot; insofar as plot is a movement towards a goal, the attainment of which is impeded by an adversary. For TzetanTodorov, a Bulgarian theorist best known for his work on narrative theory, the plot might best be understood in terms of equilibrium: equilibrium moves to disequilibrium -- perhaps the protagonist's parent dies; or they lose their job; or they find their spouse in bed with someone else -- and then disequilibrium moves back to equilibrium. Let us look at an example. Better yet: let us try and write a narrative ourselves. So we need an idea. A story about a man who lives in fits and starts: some days he exists, some days he does not. How about that? Think *The Curious Case of Benjamin Button* meets *The Time Traveller's Wife*. Or something along those lines. Okay, so we have our high concept idea. Now we need to work it out as narrative. Does the idea have legs? How might this desultory existence actually pan out? So we're talking Kafkaesque realist-surrealism. We're talking placing an absurd situation in realistic milieu. Let's think about the real-world repercussions. A man who lives on again and off again can only have on again and off again relationships. A man who lives on again and off again will struggle to meet deadlines. A man who lives on and off again will seriously question the adequacy of rationalism. Okay, how should we start it? Should we start from birth, or should we start in the middle? Should we start *abovo*, or should with start *in medias res*? I think we should start *abovo*. Why? Because it works best as a full-scale biography. At least, we need the background information before the plot gets going. We need a narrative, though. We need some kind of conflict. We need a love story, maybe. We need an antagonist. Perhaps the antagonist is his condition. It keeps on getting in his way. So he is born; and then one day he disappears from his crib; which evokes great consternation in the mother, as you can imagine; and she calls the police; and a policeman comes over; and she shows him where she last saw him; and there he is; and she blushes; and the policeman asks her kindly not to waste precious police-time in the future; and she insists that she is not crazy; and so on and so forth. What next? Next he goes to school, and the teacher thinks he's playing hooky on account of his repeated absence. He tells them about his condition, but they don't believe him; that is, not until he vanishes in the middle of a rugby match. What next? Next he asks a girl on a date; and, because of his condition, he ends up standing her up. Things like this can happen. But when does the plot actually begin? What is the plot? What is it about? So it's about being different. About not fitting into the regular space-time continuum. About being a misfit. It's a metaphor for misfitting. It's a rites of passage movie, about learning to accept oneself. To begin with, he curses his fate; in the end, he makes his peace with it. Perhaps there's a doctor who says he can fix it; who says he has localised the anomaly in the genes and can correct it, or whatever; and ultimately he decides to stay as he is. He comes to terms with his coming and going, and learns to love himself in spite of it. It's a little muddled, admittedly, but we're getting there, I feel.

So that's the substance. That's the stuff we clothe with stylish sentences. That's the archetypal structure beneath egoistic sheen. All narratives are permutations on the same theme. There exist only so many archetypes, only so many *genre*, to one of which, whether we like it or not, our narrative will belong (unless it's a generic hybrid; in which case, according to "spec screenwriter" Blake Snyder, it won't sell in a million years). But style is how one makes the Jungian archetype one's own: style is the stamp of ego on the archetype. Flaubert wanted something without external attachments; wanted an artwork all ego; wanted a mirror solely of self and not society. That's what made him so stylish. It follows, then, that the more isolated we are the more stylish we are; and the more sociable we are the better we are at telling stories. This might not be the case -- I have no empirical evidence to corroborate my assertion -- but it seems to me I'm making more sense than usual. Self is style; society is substance. Perhaps this is why minority groups -- homosexuals, for example -- are more stylish than others: i.e., because they are marginalised and more likely isolated. Society places the emphasis on the fruit of experience; the individual, conversely, on the experience in itself. The individual lives not to perpetuate the human race, not to make things better, but simply for the moment. (While I am writing this,

this is what I am thinking: I feel as though I am veering toward generalisation and abstraction. I must return to concreteness. Perhaps I should resort to a joke.) So what can we take away from our rumination on the correlation between sociability and style? Well I think it has taught us, more than anything, that our man who lives on and off again should be stylish. He should wear good clothes and make good phrases. He should disavow his philistine coevals.

Chapter 4- Success and Failure

Psychoanalysis argues that the urge to write, almost as pressing as the urge to urinate, is born out of an inaptitude for living; writers cannot live, so they live through writing. Writing is the refuge of the runt. Writers' self-esteem is low; and they need to feel as though, despite their defects, they are superior to the rest of us; so they live vicariously, through alter-egos, in a world of unreality; seduce the girls and fell the villains; win the day in a way they could not in reality. Writing, claims Freud, is a form of wish-fulfillment; a means of making a success of a difficult life. Thus, writers will often write after difficult encounters, in which they have failed to make a positive impression. They will write so as to prove that they are more than meets the eye. They will say all that they should have; all that, in the heat of the moment, their mind would not yield: they will fill the page with staircase wit. We write to show ourselves in a better light.

So the writer has low self-esteem. The writer craves praise and success, and hangs on the words of the critic. If only I can write a bestseller, one thinks, I will prove the bullies wrong; prove to them that I am not a loser; that I am, after all, a special human being. When success comes a-knocking, though – according to those who have succeeded – it is not what one expected, or might have hoped. Of course, success affects people differently; for some, it brings out the best in their writing; makes them better people: no longer bridled by jealousy, they can compliment others, and offer advice without proprietary reluctance; for some, though, it proves retarding; makes them conceited and insufferable; warps their self-image dramatically. Most of us are both harmed and hindered. I am interested more in the latter; those who have reached their goal; won the lottery; and now what? As Samuel Beckett writes, 'We are disappointed by the nullity of what we are pleased to call attainment.' For Beckett, success is a mirage; a goal which, when we reach it, moves away from us. Success is not what we expected. Success means exposure and objectification. It is amazing to think that certain writers, despite their premature success, managed to go on writing significant works. For many it proved too much. It went to their heads; weakened their wills; affected their writing negatively. If you get more pleasure from passing the parcel than composing a paragraph, then, after initial success, you will probably cease to write. Like the lead character in Sorrentino's*The Great Beauty*, you will succumb to the allure of high society.

The writer must transcend the success and failure discourse; by which I mean they must write, primarily, for the sake of writing; and give no thought to the value of their works. Once a novel is finished, then move on! Do not look back! Do not read the reviews! This might seem like strict advice – and perhaps it is – but, if one wishes to continue writing well, one must do what I tell you: one must stay away from the review section. The key to writing well is self-management. Go and stay in a faraway place, away from Twitter and Facebook, and write in the morning; read in the evening; and get a good night's sleep. We write well only when we rise above worldly affairs. We have to feel as though nothing matters, as though anything is possible. The best work is written out of such nihilistic ecstasy; which it transfuses into the readership. Success will pull us into the world. Success is a hurdle over which we must jump. Writing is a spiritual activity. Success, even more so than failure, is something to which we must inure ourselves. 'But it feels good,' you might say.

'Surely that is the whole point.' If you think like this, you cannot have really succeeded. As those who have will tell you: the initial pleasure is soon replaced by despair: you compare yourself with your former self and think, What happened to me? Working towards success – that is the real pleasure.

Failure is another matter. Failure can educate; as well as cripple irrevocably. It can be detrimental, of course. One might lose faith in oneself, and betray one's value system for the sake of improving one's mood. One does not want to feel this way again, one thinks. Failure feels bad – this goes without saying – and, as a reflex action, one will guard oneself against it; like an animal trained by pain. So one will change oneself. One will try out a different strategy. Writers in particular take failure to heart; and will see their work, henceforth, through a different filter – the filter of the critic. There is a deeper judge, however, to which we are beholden: ourselves; and the betrayal of one's value system for the sake of quick success will never result in success on the deepest of levels. Be careful not to change your work too reactively, simply because someone called it bad. Ask as many people before making fundamental amendments. If the opinions balance out, then please yourself. Writers will often say that they are their own worst critics; that if they please themselves, they will be happy; notwithstanding the general reception. This is not strictly true: we want to please others as well as ourselves – we all like to be liked – but most importantly, we want to please ourselves. Unless we can do that, we will never rest content.

Failure *can* improve us, however. It is energising: it buzzes us out of laziness. It forces us to correct our errors; reminds us that the reader cannot read our mind: forces us to explain ourselves; to think harder; to work harder. Imagine there is a trampoline below the writer: failure is falling down and bouncing back higher. You might fall so hard, of course, that you rip through the fabric. You might take to drink and wallow in your miseries. You might even derive some masochistic pleasure from it. But there are deeper joys to be had, I feel. Nothing compares to writing. Get back on the horse.

Chapter 5-The Ten Commandments of Writing

One: *Drink coffee.* This might seem like a flippant suggestion, but the effects of coffee are too good not to be exploited. Caffeine binds to adenosine receptors and prevents you from feeling fatigue. It opens up neural pathways and improves verbal recall.

Two: *Make sure your phrases follow.* In this digital age, where the majority of writing is done on word processors, it is easier than ever to chop and change one's prose. One might reread one's paragraph and see a little opening in which to insert a new idea; and then the idea might develop until the paragraph loses all coherence. Only ever write forwards.

Three: *Read extensively and intensively.* The apprentice watches the master and takes note. Plato learnt from Socrates, for example. Living in this digital age, with access to whole canons through the internet, we are spoilt for choice when it comes to teachers. Teachers are everywhere, offering their hard-won advice. The writer must be discriminating and learn from the best. Having said that, the writer can also learn a lot from bad writers as well; namely, what not to do.

Four: *Collect words*. A teacher once told me that all aspirant writers should read the dictionary. He was a man who practised what he preached: he kept the whole unabridged *Oxford English Dictionary* in his office, all twenty volumes of it, and referred to it every so often during seminars. He was a self-professed "logophile" (a lover of words), and he would come out with some of the obscurest ones you can imagine.

Five: *Have fun*. Fun is not generally something that happens on command. It seems strange to command someone to amuse themselves. But the writer must learn to have fun whenever they write. The writer must learn to do lots of things on command: must learn to conjure up different feelings – melancholy, anger, etc. – as and when they need them. Most importantly, though, the writer must learn how to have fun. You must make your writing fun, like it was when you were young. If it is not fun to write, then it is not fun to read. If you are just going through the motions, spouting platitudes and revealing as little of yourself as possible, then the reader is going to lose interest.

Six: *Be economical*. Great writers make their words count. They are better at stuffing meaning into sentences than mothers at stuffing clothes into a suitcase. They make their words work overtime. They cut out all superfluous verbiage and eschew roundabout phrasing. If you are writing an essay, cut of the stock phrases: e.g., "what is more"; "in any event"; "to this end". If you need to alert the reader to a change in direction, opt for "but" more often than "however". Keep it clean! Opt for a Germanic rather than a Latinate word! Reach into the basement of the language!

Seven: *Become a sponge of sympathy*. If you want to be a good fiction-writer, then you are going to have to collect as many character types as possible; and you are going to have to learn how different character types interact. The good fiction-writer is able to see through the eyes of someone else. Not only can they ventriloquize – the likes of Mark Twain and James Joyce were especially good at this – but they can also place themselves in the sensory field of another. In other words, they can feel through the nerves of another. Sympathising, like anything, is learnt by practice. You have to talk to as many people as possible, as openly as possible; and you have to observe as many people as possible.

Eight: *Make your details count.* If you have ever been in a creative writing workshop, you have probably heard the phrase 'Chekhov's gun'. Chekhov was a Russian dramatist, remembered for such plays as *Uncle Vanya* and *Ivanov*, to name but a few. He espoused a belief in the necessity of necessary details. For example, if an author mentions a gun in a story, then that gun should play an important role in the action. In *Ivanov*, incidentally, the gun plays a very important role.

Nine: *Never self-plagiarise.* You may get to a stage where you have amassed a fair share of verbal constructions – little turns of phrase – and, like a comedian, you begin to fill your sets with old jokes. Do not let this happen.

Ten: *Keep a notebook.* Unless you have an eidetic memory, you will need to buy a notebook. Keep it on you at all times. Record any happy sentences that occur to you. Take it with you to restaurants and record the shape of your food;

the angle of the sun on the table; the colour of the walls and the faces of the patrons; the way the sound of a saw reminds you of the breathing of a dog. This is all stuff that you can use. Unless you have an eidetic memory, then you are going to forget these details. Go out and describe what you see, and insert these descriptions into your stories. Notebooks are also good repositories for words. Write down any new words, with their meanings, and look at them as often as possible. This is how you expand your vocabulary. Record funny things that your relations say.Record dialectal utterances. Record your dreams. And, at the end of the day, commit your thoughts to a diary. Most writers keep diaries, because the pressure is off and you can write whatever you want. It is a nice change from the demands of the novel, whose every sentence, you think, must be chiselled and clear. The writer learns by writing, first and foremost; and keeping a diary, making an entrance every night, will help improve your syntax and grammar dramatically. The more you write, the better you will get. This is not strictly true. You might plateau. You might develop bad habits, even, and get worse. You have to read as well as write. Roughly speaking, however, practice makes perfect.

Conclusion

Writing is not for everyone, and it necessitates great sacrifice. Some will even tell you that writers waste their life, which might be spent (from the point of view of the selfless optimist) more usefully and (from the point of view of the selfish pessimist) more pleasurably. Seasoned writers often dissuade neophytes from continuing. Spending hours upon hours in front of a screen, in one's own company, might not seem like the most healthful of activities; might seem like a strange way to chose to spend one's time; but, as the real writer will tell you, it is not a choice: it is a kind of madness, maybe. Writers cannot help it that they feel the need to write; and that, if they do not, they will feel immensely guilty; and that, notwithstanding its downsides, it continues to appeal to them. Its negatives may even outweigh its positives. If you are a writer, though, a real writer, then you will not be able to convince yourself to stop: it is like a "bad boy" to whom you are inexorably attracted. There are many dilettantes; people who treat it like a hobby. My book is not addressed to you. My book is addressed to the people for whom; unfortunately, writing is inextricably intertwined with living; for which writing is like a "bad boy"; or, rather, a parasite, sucking up ideas like blood from the mind. We must learn to love the parasite. It is there, and it is not going to go away, so we must learn to make the best of a bad thing. We must feed it daily; but it has a discriminating palate; and it will not be satisfied with insipid prose. It will reward you when you write well, with positive chemicals; when you write badly, though, it will fill you with displeasure. So we must learn to write well.

Okay, I have sustained this ridiculous analogy for long enough. As I have instructed in the book: if you find yourself flying into abstraction, try your best to come back down to earth. Let me leave you with some honest advice: you must break as many rules as possible. See those rules above -- yes, the *Ten Commandments of Writing* -- well, you should try and break as many of these as possible. The art of great writing is breaking the rules and getting away with it. You might as well try and be great: there are enough good books in the world; and there are enough average books in the world. My advice to you -- though I concede it is irresponsible -- is to take risks. Be wanton! You will either write something unreadable or something unique.

Of course, I would be lying if I said that I do not think there is something noble about writing. Like most people, I have an irrational respect for the great writer. Maybe it is wrong of us to apotheosize these "geniuses"; but maybe there *is* a hint of truth in the romantic idea of genius. Sometimes an afflatus comes upon us, is blown into us, and we write into reality something distinct from our history of experience. Writing can educate the writer, first and foremost. As the Frenchman Maurice Merleau-Ponty puts it, 'My own words take me by surprise and teach me what to think.' I echo this Frenchman's sentiment. This makes writing worthwhile.

We are nearing the end now. This -- alas! -- shall be the final paragraph of my humble little eBook. We shall soon part company; I will cease to make sounds in your mind; you will find yourself alone; and you will have to carry on with the business of living. I hope you have enjoyed reading as much as I have enjoyed writing. Generally the one corresponds to the other. I hope it has informed you; and, above all, I hope it has delighted you. Please feel free to leave write a review, and tell us what you think! If I can leave you with one thought, it is this: writing should be pleasurable. If it is not, if it has become laborious for you, then remember what it was like when you were a child. We must constantly self-infantilize: we must maintain a childish delight in the act of imagining; we must maintain a childish curiosity about the world. The writer must fight for delight -- that is, the pleasure of writing does not always yield itself readily -- but the writer will agree with me, I am sure, that there are few things more delightful in this life, in this crazy game of life, than the act of writing.